FINISHING LINE PRESS

www.finishinglinepress.com

being from being broke open

poems by

Marcia Casey

Finishing Line Press
Georgetown, Kentucky

being from being broke open

ACKNOWLEDGMENTS

The author would like to thank the editors of publications in which the
following poems have previously appeared, some in slightly different form:

"Storks" in Renee Askins' *Shadow Mountain: A Memoir of Wolves, a Woman,
and the Wild,*
"Chorus for a Poetics of Matter" as part of an essay, "The Human: A Poetics
of Matter" in *Jacket Magazine*
"in the studio: life drawing" was part of a reading and exhibit entitled
"Nekkid," a collaboration between the Life Drawing class and the poets
of Jackson Hole Writers, at the Jackson Hole Center for the Arts Gallery,
February 5-March 15, 2010
"Two Women Part at Dusk" in Jeopardy, Western Washington University
"Building the Ark," "Storks," "Bird-Wise," "what breaks," "Walking with
Grief," "Chorus for a Poetics of Matter," and "in the studio: life drawing"
individually in various issues of *The Labyrinth: St. Luke & St. Stephen Review*

The author would also like to thank Cheryl Aden, Denise Casey and Linnea
Harper for their invaluable editorial assistance. And deepest gratitude to
Cheryl also for her stunning cover photograph.

Publisher: Leah Huete de Maines
Editor: Christen Kincaid
Cover Art: "Diurnal Rebirth" ©2016 Cheryl Aden
Author Photo: Harmony Griffith
Cover Design: Elizabeth Maines McCleavy

Order online: www.finishinglinepress.com
also available on amazon.com

Author inquiries and mail orders:
Finishing Line Press
PO Box 1626
Georgetown, Kentucky 40324
USA

Contents

For my cornerstones
Denise, Evanne, Cheryl, and Laurie

And for the one who brought me to grace
Judith +

Prologue

...the sea anemone dreams of something,
filtering the sea water thru its body...
                    George Oppen

1 Substance

Vivid, translucent,
the sea floor's sinuous frond
sifts the undulant
tide. Mindless, she fingers
its shifting
substance. She muses—
her sensitive hackles
bristle and hush with each
swerve
in the pull of the waves.
In the hollow of her
muscular trunk, the notion
of hunger, or some unknown
yearning, stirs.
She mulls—
                    whisk of fin, snap of synapse, she
clasps her prey. In the vessel
of her body
she slowly ingests
this day's catch: *shiver*
                           intuition
                           flesh

2 Inkling

In the slow swirl, a ripple
trips his senses—his tentacles sheer
to a singular angle
on the axis of discerning:
he's intent on one
dark inkling—a portent of form
flickering in the phosphorescent
wake of the sea-wind...

3 Stance

Her pedestal, shimmering, sheer
ring of cleaving, clings
unwavering to stone. From this shore
of devotion
she flings her
halo of sentience
headlong. Utterly open,
she's swept on tumult
toward sundering—transfixed
on the abyss
she bears the unfathomable
stance of the saint—absolute
anchor and absolute
abandon.

4 Act

In the heart of profusion, he bows
to his task: sensing
the path of grace. He must
speak or make
    an immaculate act
and move
with its nuance.
He sets his tentacles
to ground to begin
the tricky, deliberate arc of this
somersault...

5. Turbulence

In her crystal pool, the subtlest
eddies trouble
her limbs—undercurrents,
semblances surge
and fade, Poseidon's trident flashes
and vanishes—she shudders
in wonder
and fear. Sibilant whispers
haunt what
she cannot hear, Cassandra
drowned in echo
and tidal
hiss—elusive…
As she strains
to listen, her head
of tentacles
seethes
like snakes.

6 Apogee

Men probe
her glistening, primitive
ganglia, extracting
secrets
from her freakish,
unspeakable form.
They return to their wooden
craft, to tally and define.
In the night, though, rocking
they relinquish the specific,
and soften
and drift
in the stream of her glimmering
realm: science dissolves
into spiral and curl and
in the deep they see,
healed of fractions, her
whole. O then
the siren
begins to unveil
the psalm of her infinite
name, singing
elegans
magnifica
mirabilis...

7. Center

Fimbria flaring, they bloom,
rapt, their fluent
fringes
supplicant to the sea. The end of each
extremity opens: in the holy
confusion, communion, they come to be
      porous
      luminous
      illumined
in their brilliant
raiment, matter.

Ocean

We are what the seas
have made us
longingly immense
　　　　Lorine Niedecker

O slow tolling of the Ocean
washing through us
O infinite glittering
sorrow of sands soughing
in our seabed

　　　　　Mother, she stills us
rocking stroking poring over
our small wounds
while fathomless grief
heaves in her abyss, undertow's
shudder we suckle
in the surf of
her ceaseless murmur
her
　　　hush…
　　　　　　hush…
　　　　　　　　　hush…

Building the Ark

Noah, gathering
lumber and hammers, must have known
it was something big.
Troubled, he tried
to keep his mind
on the parts he knew he could do—measuring,
sawing, planing, joining—the practical
tasks that make
the hull. But he couldn't
not see how the whole
took shape, not feel the unfathomable
cavern in the hold
bowing the screeching wood
from within—he ached
to stop his ears, stop
short of begging
what wood could bear, stop
terror... He bent
nearer his work, honed
one longing: to be able
to set the next
nail true.

Storks

On this cold night
winter's last rally
rakes across the fledgling breast
of spring like claws: the last
white bear turns, hungering,
northward.

We put on layers of sweaters again
and light a circle of lamps
deep in the heart of the house. But
we are restless, keep listening.
You are the first to get up.
You pace a few silent steps,
then go. Upstairs I find you
perched at the window,
an early stork
staring from the slender chimney
of your bones down
at icy slivers of teeth
slicing into tender garden growth.

Without thinking,
we gather the afghans
and carefully fold our long limbs
down into them.
With a soft ritual clicking of bills,
necks twining, wings rising,
we begin
the ancient migration
back to the place
of our birth.

Bird-Wise

While all around him, wrangling
for purchase, the fractious world
turns, *he* turns
counter to it. His boy's body
capering bird-wise
crooks its elbows haphazardly up—and the opening
ambushes him! Sweeps him into
an involution so profound
his dabbling spins into dance
and the Wild Bird
spirals free!

Keepsake

Your baby teeth tick
inside a tiny jar, glimmer,
almost grimace, almost
grin... I shake them
loose into tinkle and glitter,
a clatter of ancient
baby laughter—Oh! Sharp sweet bite
tender old wound
        again

    for Evanne

Something Throngs in Your Ears and It's Night

You wake.
The man downstairs is ranting again.
He's turned up the set: hymns
mix with his dark harangue.
You can't see the angels
but feel their static
shivery, fractured,
strung on the air.

Mud Island

A wind from the north
forms crusts of ice
along the shore. The river
shivers southward
as I stand beneath the leafless trees
staring, numb.
A bare black hump
sticks up midstream,
mud island, hunchback
drowned face-down,
caught in the throat
of the skittering river.
Raw mud, drenched with waves,
freezes in the bitter air.
Brittle, distant cries of geese
scatter south: they're calling me.
I stand here thin and blue, a heron,
my wings hung wrong, awkward,
unable to move.
They say in time
this unwieldy grief will dissolve,
drifting away like silt to the sea,
growing smooth, sleek,
light like a feather…
But winter is coming.
Ice grips the river,
stranding, rigid,
two huge, aberrant corpses.

what breaks

Are cries nothing?
Octavio Paz

the wound breaks
what's integral
open, rends
wholeness, renders its
being
broken

speech breaks, fracturing
sentence, sense—the senselessness we
all speak breaks into
being from being
broke open

what breaks breaks
mercy
open in us, new
wound for the wounded
being we tend
with what
seeps from these cracks—our serum
tears   our
salve   love

for LG

Passage

In the rite of The Reconciliation of a Penitent
the most difficult moment was not
the Confession, the exposing
before all
of my utter, my naked
disgrace as a human being—no, it was
later... after... when I tucked you
in effigy

> *small rosebud face*
> *set in a skeleton*
> *of live olive twigs,*
> *nestled in the fleece I'd saved*
> *from our newborn lambs*

into the swaddling blanket
I made you
like any mother would
layered from remnants of her own
memoir

> *the flowered burgundy rayon*
> *I'd used as a curtain in that tiny apartment*
> *Katharine found me in Bellingham;*
> *the subtly-patterned off-white satin*
> *I'd made into a ring-bearer pillow*
> *for the wedding of Laurie and Rosean;*
> *and, cached between them, the softest,*
> *most intimate flannel from my favorite*
> *nightgown, that had lain, dark after dark*
> *against my own skin*

and pulled the gold cord more snugly
around the beloved
bundle of you
to keep you
in the flimsy, clumsy
cat's cradle of my love
even as I lifted you
onto the altar
to give you
away again,
this time for good

for Olive Rose

Walking with Grief

In the garden, come evening
you walk, accompanied
by grief—weighty, unwieldy
like a child in your arms who lurches
to reach for some
leaf   flicker of bird   rupture of light
then settles back
for a liminal moment—as a heart might
pause to restore its own rhythm—only to turn
and plunge abruptly
into the hollow
of your chest, where this ungovernable
being grips you with its twist of beauty
so fervently you're held—healed—for a moment...
then move on, bound
through the quiet
channel of evening
which draws you
together beneath
the dark branching
of trees

Prayer to the Pleiades

Lovely circle
in the studded sky, keep us
safe. Teach us faith,
halo, between
the eternal wheeling
of god and beast and the infinite
spin of space. Through war
and fear, touch our faces
with your ancient, naked grace.

Chorus for a Poetics of Matter: a cento

I have to trust what was given
to me... the stars
over the shadowless mountain / Being
itself / beings... flung free into nothing other
than a drawing toward the center / an instinctive
tendency
to acquire an art / to travel the deeps of air
with no fear / listening
to matter / what does it
not remember
in its night
and silence / the soundness
of worldly existence—this
is what is
to be said / to stir words
into thoughts like things / sacred
things I had to arrange / the weaving
of words / to follow their
wishes / what's your urgent charge, if not
transformation / the eyes of fire
the nostrils of air, the mouth of water
the beard of the
earth / Infernal Genius / speak
and testify / who goes there
hankering, gross, mystical, nude / more beautiful
after every wound /
one
and another
and another / whoever
we finally may be / we
build and we come and we reach / but
the saying is hard—the hard thing
is to accomplish
existence / we say its name / Oh!...
in a way that
things themselves never

dreamed of /
just so /
so it might
matter

Sources of the quotes in "Chorus for a Poetics of Matter" in order:

WS Merwin / Annie Dillard / Martin Heidegger /
Charles Darwin / Eleni Sikelianos / Cecilia Vicuña /
WS Merwin / Martin Heidegger / Eleni Sikelianos /
Cecilia Vicuña / Cecilia Vicuña / Cecilia Vicuña /
Rainer Maria Rilke / William Blake / William Blake /
Rainer Maria Rilke / Walt Whitman / WS Merwin /
Juliana Spahr / Rainer Maria Rilke / Juliana Spahr /
Martin Heidegger / Marcia Casey / Rainer Maria Rilke /
Laurie Gudim / Juliana Spahr

in the studio: life drawing

This is what we do
when we do what
we are...
                        Matthew Shenoda

1 convening

we shed all
coats, conceits, connections
the usual tangles
at the door—here
we enter the spare
studio, its single
endeavor a fuse
lit, transfixing
        beholder   beheld

2 conundrum

his inwardness
centers us—pegged
as human
by the clench in
the crux of his
brow, the model
yet stands forth as
object, sans
person—we, too, cede
ourselves   find ourselves
gathered in the remote
cosmos of his face

3 scope

we pore over
arc tic knuckle
this structure of reach, twist
angle and splay, which
turns on some unseen
axis: in each between us shadow
and sheen are tenderly
rendered—seer and seen, we
school ourselves in
being   a thing
inexplicably
pinioned with doing,
this seeing and making
kindle   combustion
encumbered   sprung

4 inflection

the difficult
draws us—the oblique
task of arresting
what moves us   *a singular*
                   arc of wrist   this
infinitesimal gesture   inflected
in draft upon draft, a sheaf of small
fidelities deepening   at moments
opening   the body   suddenly
come true

5 notch

into the flare and lift
of clavicles, the neck's
strong descending tendons
countersink   lock   the crucial
notch anchors the scaffold
from which the body elaborates,
the platform from which the ponderous
head considers   yet at its root
blooms a small cleft
where the sturdy body stands
ajar—in its hollow quiver
flickers of breath   the quick
leaps that impel
our work   sheer prayers
of ache and amaze

Two Women Part at Dusk

As the sun slips down
we turn
                        back to dusk:
leaves open
their oval wells,
the dark trees
spill together, and night
swirls
around our waists.

We kiss:
                        cool moths
flutter
from the dust.

We part
                        as ripples
into our halo
of waters.

      for KS

Marcia Casey earned her BA in Creative Writing from Fairhaven College and her MFA from Goddard College. Her poetry received an Honorable Mention in the Wyoming Arts Council's 2010 Neltje Blanchan Writing Award for poetry informed by a relationship with the natural world. Her poems have also received prizes at the Northwest Poets Concord in Newport, Oregon, in 2012 and 2014.

She has taught community workshops and an outreach program in poetry for students with disabilities under the auspices of the Jackson Hole Writers.

Her essay, "The Human: A Poetics of Matter," appeared in *Jacket Magazine*; her poems have previously appeared in *Wisconsin Academy Review, Jeopardy, Pitkin Review*, and the *Jackson Hole Review*. She currently lives on the Oregon coast and edits a local creative arts publication called *The Labyrinth*.